The Simple Wealth Guide

R RADHAKRISHNAN

Published by Radhakrishnan R, 2024.

While every precaution has been taken in the preparation of this book, the publisher assumes no responsibility for errors or omissions, or for damages resulting from the use of the information contained herein.

THE SIMPLE WEALTH GUIDE

First edition. October 16, 2024.

ISBN: 979-8227680860

Written by R RADHAKRISHNAN.

To my kids

Aishwariya

and

Avaneesh

Preface

I worked in a salaried job but have been investing for decades now. Most of the investing decisions were haphazard and many a time taken based on a friend, a relative or so called "financial or insurance advisors."

The result was that my investments were not growing the way they should. Over the years, I realised I should not depend on these sorts of advice but make my own decisions.

I was not mathematically inclined and so felt investment was not my cup of tea. But after a couple of unpleasant experiences began to read and learn a bit more.

Over the years, I put my little learning to use, and the results were satisfactory. My investments helped me in educating my children, buy a house and have a comfortable life.

As my kids grew up, they asked me for financial advice and when I spoke to them; I realised I knew a bit more than many people.

I wrote a small write up for my kids to read when they are free so that they could know the basics and make more informed decisions rather than make the same mistakes I did.

This small book is but an expansion of what I wrote for my kids. It is an attempt to explain the basics of investment to them so that can take a more informed decision.

In today's connected world, there is a surfeit of information which is confusing. I have tried to keep it simple, cutting the fluff so that only the relevant information is there. I hope this book is useful in your journey.

R.Radhakrishnan

R RADHAKRISHNAN

Ernakulam

July 2024.

Introduction:

In today's fast-paced world, achieving financial security and independence is more important than ever. With so many investment options available, it can feel overwhelming, especially for beginners. Whether you want to retire early, buy your dream home, or simply feel secure about your financial future, investing wisely is key to making your dreams come true.

Welcome to The Simple Wealth Guide to financial freedom and prosperity. This book simplifies investing and gives you the knowledge, tools, and strategies to build a sound foundation for wealth creation.

Why is investing important? Simply saving money is not enough to secure your financial future. In today's low-interest-rate environment, keeping your money in a savings account can make it lose value over time due to inflation. Investing, however, allows your money to grow by working for you.

For beginners, investing can seem intimidating with its unfamiliar terms, complex financial instruments, and endless choices. That is where this book comes in. We have condensed decades of investment experience into an easy-to-understand guide for beginners.

This book is your roadmap to understanding the basics of investing, from stocks, bonds, and mutual funds to more advanced concepts like asset allocation, diversification, and risk management. With it, you can plan your own step-by-step personalized investment plan based on your financial goals, risk tolerance, and time horizon.

This book is more than just a theoretical guide—it is a practical toolkit with actionable strategies, real-world examples, and insights to help you plan your investments. This is a book for beginners to understand the basics of investments.

If you are ready to take control of your financial future, grow your wealth, and live life on your own terms, then this is the book for you. Let us start this journey together and unlock a brighter, more prosperous future.

All investments come with a risk. You need to understand the basics so that you understand the risks and can take an informed decision.

This book does not promise to make you a millionaire overnight. It will not tell you where to invest or when to invest. There are no shortcuts to good investments. You need to understand the basics, create your investment plan, and then decide what will work best for you. This book will help you understand the basics so that you will be able to take an informed decision for your future.

The risks are there, but a sound investment plan will reduce the risks and the fruits you will enjoy will be sweeter and better.

Finally, the decision is yours to make as the risks and the fruits both belong to you. You can jump in blindly or take informed decisions.

Why should you pursue wealth?

In Hinduism, **Artha** refers to pursuing material wealth and prosperity. It involves the responsible accumulation of resources and economic well-being.

Wealth is essential for leading a comfortable life and supporting ourselves and our family. The scriptures emphasize it should be pursued with integrity and in harmony with **Dharma**—the righteous path[1].

The pursuit of Artha is closely tied to the activities of statecraft, which maintain social order and prevent anarchy.

Along with Dharma, Artha, Kama, and **Moksha** are three fundamental pursuits in Hindu philosophy, collectively known as **Purusharthas.**

Artha (Material Wealth and Prosperity):

Artha refers to the pursuit of material well-being, wealth, and economic prosperity.

It encompasses gaining resources, financial stability, and fulfilling basic needs.

Artha is essential for leading a comfortable life and supporting oneself and one's family.

However, it should be pursued with integrity and in harmony with Dharma (righteousness).

Kama (Desire and Pleasure):

Kama represents the pursuit of desires, pleasure, and sensual enjoyment.

It includes emotional fulfilment, love, aesthetics, and artistic expression.

---

1. _https://www.britannica.com/topic/artha_

Kama is not merely about physical pleasure; it also encompasses intellectual and emotional satisfaction.

When pursued within ethical boundaries, Kama contributes to a balanced and harmonious life.

Moksha (Liberation or Spiritual Enlightenment):

Moksha is the ultimate goal of human existence.

It transcends the cycle of birth and rebirth (samsara) and leads to liberation from suffering.

Achieving Moksha involves realizing one's true nature (Atman) and merging with the universal consciousness (Brahman).

Practices such as meditation, self-realization, and detachment from worldly attachments lead to Moksha.

Wealth provides the foundation for a stable life.

Kama adds richness and joy, and Moksha leads to spiritual liberation.

Balancing these pursuits is essential for a meaningful existence.

Thus, pursuing wealth ethically is part of your spiritual growth too, so you do not have to feel guilty about it, but it is your duty. Go for it, says the sacred books!

Let us chat about investments and all that stuff.

1. *What is investment?*

Investment is the act of putting your money into assets with the expectation of earning a profit or gaining some form of return in the future. The goal of investing is to grow your wealth.

2. *Why should you invest?*

Investing allows your money to work for you and has the potential to generate returns higher than what you could earn by simply saving your money in a bank account. It helps you build wealth, achieve financial goals like buying a house or retiring comfortably, and beat inflation.

3. *Basic investment terminology:*

Fixed Deposits (FDs): Fixed deposits are a type of investment offered by banks and financial institutions. When you invest in an FD, you are lending money to the bank for a fixed period at a predetermined interest rate. At the end of the tenure, you receive the principal amount along with the interest earned.

Stocks: When you buy a stock, you are buying a small piece of ownership in a company.

Bonds: Bonds are loans you give to governments or corporations. In return, they promise to pay you back the amount you loaned, plus interest.

Mutual funds: These are investment vehicles that pool money from many investors to invest in a diversified portfolio of stocks, bonds, or other assets.

ETFs (Exchange-Traded Funds): Like mutual funds, but they trade on stock exchanges, like individual stocks.

Diversification: Spreading your investments across different types of assets to reduce risk.

Risk: The possibility of losing money on an investment. Higher returns come with higher risk.

Return: The profit or loss generated by an investment over a certain period, usually expressed as a percentage.

Portfolio: The collection of all your investments. You can have your main portfolio containing all your investments and there can be dedicated portfolios like your stock portfolio, your mutual fund portfolio, bond portfolio etc. so that you can track each group of investments as well. The risk factors and the growth factors will also change depending on what type of investment it is.

4. Methods of investing:

Long-term investing: Buying and holding investments for an extended period, usually years or decades, to benefit.

Short-term trading: Buying and selling assets over shorter periods, often trying to profit from market fluctuations.

Passive investing: Investing in index funds or ETFs that track a market index, like the S&P 500, and aiming to match its performance.

Active investing: Trying to outperform the market by selecting individual stocks or timing the market.

5. How to get started:

Set financial goals: Determine what you want to achieve through investing.

Educate yourself: Learn about different investment options, strategies, and risks.

Start small: Begin with an amount you are comfortable with and gradually increase your investments.

Diversify: Spread your investments across different asset classes to reduce risk.

Consider seeking professional advice, especially if you are unsure about where to start or how to manage your investments.

Remember, investing is a journey, not a sprint. It is important to stay patient, stay informed, and be prepared to adapt your strategy as your financial situation and goals evolve. Remember, the tortoise from the story, slow and steady, wins the race.

Assets and what do they mean in financial terms?

Let us see what we mean by assets and how they are important in our pursuit of wealth.

Assets refer to resources with economic value that are owned or controlled by individuals, companies, or countries, with the expectation of future benefits.

Types of Assets:

Current Assets: These are short-term economic resources expected to be converted into cash or consumed within one year. Examples include cash, accounts receivable, physical inventory, and prepaid expenses.

Fixed Assets: Fixed assets have an expected life of more than a year and include items like plants, equipment, and buildings. Depreciation adjustments are made for fixed assets as they age.

Financial Assets: These are non-physical assets whose value comes from contractual claims. Examples include stocks, bonds, mutual funds, and bank deposits[1].

Intangible Assets: These have monetary value but lack physical substance. Examples include copyrights, patents, trademarks, and goodwill.

Purpose of Assets:

Assets may generate cash flow, reduce expenses, or improve sales.

They can be either tangible (like machinery or real estate) or intangible (like intellectual property).

---

1. https://www.investopedia.com/terms/a/asset.asp

For businesses, assets are reported on the company's balance sheet.

Remember that assets play a crucial role in financial planning and wealth management.

Let us also talk a bit about liabilities, as they also affect our wealth accumulation.

Assets and **liabilities** are fundamental concepts in finance and accounting, representing what a business or individual owns and owes, respectively. Here are the key differences:

- **Assets**: Resources owned by a business or individual that provide future economic benefits. Examples include cash, inventory, property, and investments.
- **Liabilities**: Obligations or debts that a business or individual owes to others. Examples include loans, accounts payable, mortgages, and other debts.

Impact on Financial Health:

- **Assets**: Add value to the business or individual by generating income or providing future benefits.
- **Liabilities**: Subtract from the value as they represent obligations that must be paid off.

Balance Sheet Representation:

- **Assets**: Listed on the left side or top section of the balance sheet.
- **Liabilities**: Listed on the right side or bottom section of the balance sheet.

Types:

- **Assets**: Can be current (short term) or fixed (long term), tangible or intangible.
- **Liabilities**: Can be current (short-term) or long term.

Understanding the balance between assets and liabilities is crucial for assessing financial stability and making informed financial decisions.

The power of compounding.

Let me tell you a story from ancient India.

Muni Bhardwaj, the rishi who invented chess, was in the court of a king who was proud of his wealth. The King asked the Rishi to ask for anything he desired but the rishi declined. The king was insistent, so the Rishi asked for grains of rice. But the condition was that the rice would be given based on the chessboard. On the first square there would be one grain of rice, on the second square there would be two grains and on the third square there would be four grains and on the fourth square there would be eight grains of rice. So, it would go on doubling the number of grains as you progressed from one square to another. Simple, thought the king. We will not go into the mathematics involved as we want to simplify and demystify investment.

But the total number of grains required to fill all the squares on a chessboard is 18,446,744,073,709,551,615.

The number 18,446,744,073,709,551,615 is pronounced as "eighteen quintillion, four hundred forty-six quadrillion, seven hundred forty-four trillion, seventy-three billion, seven hundred nine million, five hundred fifty-one thousand, six hundred fifteen." Quite a mouthful, isn't it?

Now that is a huge number, and the granary of the king did not have that quantity of rice. We are not concerned about the moral of the story, but rather the exponential increase in the number of grains.

Compounding works similarly and now you can appreciate the power of compounding.

Compounding in financial terms refers to the process where an asset's earnings—whether from capital gains or interest—are reinvested to generate additional earnings. Here are the key points:

Interest on Interest:

Compounding magnifies returns because it credits interest not only to the initial principal but also to the accumulated interest from the preceding periods.

This phenomenon is often called the "miracle of compounding."

Frequency and Types:

Financial institutions use compounding periods (e.g., annual, monthly, or daily) when crediting compound interest.

It occurs naturally in savings accounts, Provident fund accounts and some dividend-yielding investments.

Remember, compounding plays a crucial role in finance, leading to the exponential growth of assets or capital.

Let us look at some ways that we can use this growth mantra.

Compounding is the process where the value of an investment grows exponentially over time as you earn returns not just on your initial investment, but also on the returns generated in previous periods. In simpler terms, it is like earning interest on your interest.

How can compounding be harnessed to build a corpus over time?

Let us look at an example: Imagine you invest Rs.1,000 in an FD that offers an annual interest rate of 5% compounded annually. After the first year, you will have Rs 1,050 (1,000 + 5% interest). Now, in the second year, you are not just earning interest on your initial Rs.1,000 but on Rs1,050. So, you will earn Rs. 52.50 in interest, bringing your total to Rs.1,102.50. This process continues year after year.

The longer you keep your money invested, the more powerful compounding becomes. Over time, your money grows not just linearly, but exponentially. So, starting to invest early is crucial because it gives your money more time to compound. But you can use it at any stage of your life.

Building a corpus with compounding:

Let us say you invest Rs 100 per month in an investment vehicle that offers an average annual return of 8%, compounded monthly. Here is how your investment could grow over time:

After 10 years: Approximately Rs. 18,679

After 20 years: Approximately Rs. 57,275

After 30 years: Approximately Rs.163,985

As you can see, even though you have only invested Rs 36,000 over 30 years (Rs.100 per month for 360 months), the power of compounding has turned it into a substantial amount.

Tips for harnessing the power of compounding:

Start investing early to maximize the time your money has to compound.

Reinvest your earnings to allow them to compound further.

Be patient and consistent with your investments.

Choose investment vehicles that offer compound interest, like PF accounts, stocks, mutual funds, or retirement accounts.

By understanding and harnessing the power of compounding, you can build a significant corpus over time, helping you achieve your financial goals and secure your future.

Stocks and how stocks can help build wealth:

Stocks represent ownership in a company. When you buy stocks, you are buying shares of that company, making you a partial owner. Stocks are traded on stock exchanges like the New York Stock Exchange (NYSE) or the Nasdaq, The National Stock Exchange of India (Nifty) or the Bombay Stock Exchange (The Sensex)

1.Capital appreciation: If the value of the company grows over time, the price of its stock increases as well. This allows you to sell your shares at a higher price, making a profit.

2. Dividend income: Some companies pay a portion of their profits to shareholders in the form of dividends. Investing in dividend-paying stocks can provide a steady stream of income.

Fundamentals to keep in mind while investing in stocks:

1. Research: Understand the company you are investing in, including its business model, financial health, management team, and competitive advantage.

2. Diversification: Do not put all your money into just one or a few stocks. Diversify your portfolio across different industries and types of stocks to reduce risk. Remember, putting all your eggs in one basket increase the risk of breakage.

3. Risk tolerance: Be aware of your risk tolerance and invest accordingly. Stocks can be volatile, so be prepared for fluctuations in the market. Be realistic, you cannot make a profit with all your stock investments,

sometimes you need to cut your losses and exit from a stock to reduce further losses.

4. Long-term perspective: Investing in stocks is a long-term endeavour. Try to avoid reacting to short-term market fluctuations and focus on the company's long-term potential.

Pros of investing in stocks:

1. Potential for high returns: Stocks have a higher risk but historically have provided higher returns compared to other asset classes, like bonds or cash, over the long term.

2. Ownership: Buying stocks means owning a part of a company, giving you a stake in its success.

3. Liquidity: Stocks are highly liquid investments, meaning you can easily buy and sell them on the stock exchange. But check whether it is traded on a regular basis. Some stocks may not be traded regularly, or you may not find a buyer at the price you ask for.

Cons of investing in stocks:

1. Risk: Stocks can be volatile, and there is a risk of losing money, especially in the short term.

2. Market fluctuations: Stock prices can be influenced by several factors, including economic conditions, company performance, and investor sentiment.

3. Lack of control: As a minor shareholder, you have limited control over the company's decisions and management.

4. Dividend uncertainty: Not all stocks pay dividends, and dividend payments can vary or be cut depending on the company's performance.

Overall, investing in stocks can be an effective way to build wealth over time, but it is important to do your research, diversify your portfolio, and be prepared to ride out market fluctuations.

There are several key ratios that investors use to analyse stocks. Each ratio provides different insights into various aspects of a company's financial performance and health. Here are some of the most used ratios and their significance:

1. Price-to-Earnings (P/E) Ratio:

Significance: The P/E ratio compares a company's current stock price to its earnings per share (EPS). It helps investors assess whether a stock is undervalued, overvalued, or fairly valued relative to its earnings. It shows how much time it will take to get your original investment back at current prices and current earning levels of the stock.

Formula: P/E Ratio = Stock Price / Earnings per Share

2. Price-to-Book (P/B) Ratio:

Significance: The P/B ratio compares a company's market value (its stock price) to its book value (total assets minus total liabilities). It shows whether a stock is undervalued or overvalued relative to its assets.

Formula: P/B Ratio = Stock Price / (Total Assets - Total Liabilities)

3. Debt-to-Equity (D/E) Ratio:

Significance: The D/E ratio measures a company's financial leverage by comparing its total debt to its shareholders' equity. It helps investors assess the company's risk level and ability to meet its financial obligations.

Formula: D/E Ratio = Total Debt / Shareholders' Equity

4. Return on Equity (ROE):

Significance: ROE measures a company's profitability by comparing its net income to its shareholders' equity. It shows how effectively the company is using its equity to generate profits.

Formula: ROE = Net Income / Shareholders' Equity

5. Earnings Per Share (EPS):

Significance: EPS measures a company's profitability by dividing its net income by the number of outstanding shares. It helps investors evaluate a company's earnings on a per-share basis.

Formula: EPS = Net Income / Number of Outstanding Shares

6. Dividend Yield:

Significance: Dividend yield measures the percentage return on a stock's dividend payments relative to its current market price. It helps investors assess the income potential of dividend-paying stocks.

Formula: Dividend Yield = Annual Dividend Per Share / Stock Price

7. Gross Margin:

Significance: Gross margin measures the percentage of revenue that exceeds the cost of goods sold. It helps investors assess a company's profitability and efficiency in producing goods or services.

Formula: Gross Margin = (Revenue - Cost of Goods Sold) / Revenue

8. Current Ratio:

Significance: The current ratio measures a company's ability to pay its short-term liabilities with its short-term assets. It helps investors assess the company's liquidity and financial health.

Formula: Current Ratio = Current Assets / Current Liabilities

These ratios are just a few of the many metrics investors use to analyse stocks. By understanding and interpreting these ratios, investors can make more informed decisions about which stocks to buy, hold, or sell.

You can find these ratios for any company online as they will normally be in the public domain. Your stockbroking application or website will also have these for most companies that are listed.

Large cap, mid-cap, and small cap are terms used to categorize companies based on their market capitalization, which is the total value of a company's outstanding shares of stock. Here is an overview of each:

1. Large-Cap Stocks:

Large-cap stocks are issued by large, well-established companies with a market capitalization typically greater than $10 billion.

These companies are often industry leaders with a long history of stable performance and typically have a global presence.

Large-cap stocks are considered relatively stable and less volatile compared to mid-cap and small-cap stocks.

Investors often turn to large-cap stocks for stability and income generation, as many large companies pay dividends.

2. Mid-cap Stocks:

Mid-cap stocks are issued by companies with a market capitalization ranging from $2 billion to $10 billion.

These companies are often in a phase of growth and expansion, with the potential for higher returns compared to large-cap stocks.

Mid-cap stocks may offer a balance between stability and growth potential, as they are not as established as large cap companies but are not as risky as small cap companies.

Investors interested in moderate growth potential and willing to accept higher risk often consider mid-cap stocks.

3. Small-Cap Stocks:

Small-cap stocks are issued by companies with a market capitalization typically below $2 billion.

These companies are often newer, less established, and may operate in niche markets or emerging industries.

Small-cap stocks have the potential for significant growth, but they also are more volatile and carry higher risk compared to large and mid-cap stocks.

Investors seeking higher growth potential and willing to tolerate greater volatility may invest in small-cap stocks.

Investors often consider their risk tolerance, investment objectives, and time horizon when deciding whether to invest in large cap, mid-cap, or small-cap stocks.

Large-cap stocks are typically more suitable for conservative investors seeking stability, while mid-cap and small-cap stocks may appeal to investors seeking higher growth potential, albeit with higher risk. Diversification across different market capitalizations can also help manage overall portfolio risk.

What is investment profile?

An investment profile, also known as an investor profile or risk profile, is a description of an individual's investment objectives, risk tolerance, time horizon, and financial situation. It helps investors and financial advisors determine the most suitable investment strategy and asset allocation based on their unique circumstances. Several factors contribute to determining an individual's investment profile:

1. Investment Objectives:

Investment objectives reflect what an investor aims to achieve through their investments. Common objectives include capital preservation, income generation, capital appreciation, and wealth accumulation for specific goals such as retirement, education, or purchasing a home.

2. Risk Tolerance:

Risk tolerance refers to an investor's ability and willingness to withstand fluctuations in the value of their investments. It is influenced by factors such as age, income, investment experience, financial goals, time horizon, and emotional temperament. Some investors are comfortable with higher levels of risk in pursuit of potentially higher returns, while others prefer lower-risk investments to preserve capital.

3. Time Horizon:

Time horizon is the time an investor expects to hold their investments before needing to access the funds for a specific financial goal or milestone. Investors with longer time horizons, such as those saving for retirement or a child's education, may have greater flexibility to tolerate short-term market fluctuations and pursue high-risk, high-return investments. Conversely, investors with shorter time horizons may prefer lower-risk investments to protect against potential losses near their goal deadlines.

4. Financial Situation:

An investor's financial situation, including income, expenses, assets, liabilities, and liquidity needs, plays a significant role in determining their investment profile. Factors such as employment stability, debt level, emergency savings, and overall financial health influence an investor's capacity to take on investment risk and commit funds to various investment vehicles.

5. Knowledge and Experience:

An investor's knowledge of financial markets, investment products, and investment strategies, as well as their past investment experience, can shape their investment profile. Novice investors may prefer simpler, more straightforward investments, while seasoned investors may be comfortable with complex strategies and alternative investments.

6. Ethical and Social Considerations:

Some investors may have specific ethical, social, or environmental criteria that guide their investment decisions. They may prioritize investing in companies or funds that align with their values or exclude certain industries or practices from their portfolios.

By considering these factors, investors and financial professionals can create customized investment profiles tailored to individual needs, preferences, and circumstances. This helps ensure that investment strategies align with investors' goals and risk tolerances, enhancing the likelihood of achieving long-term financial success.

You should periodically review your profile as your goals and ideas change. There is no one rule or a set profile. You should finally invest as per your comfort levels.

What is insurance and is it an investment?

Insurance serves primarily as a risk management tool rather than an investment vehicle.

While some insurance products offer a cash value component or investment feature, their primary purpose is to provide financial protection against specific risks, such as loss of income due to disability, medical expenses, property damage, or death. However, certain insurance products, such as permanent life insurance policies like whole life or universal life, include savings or investment component alongside the insurance coverage.

When purchasing insurance, whether it includes an investment component, there are several key factors to consider:

1. Coverage Needs:

Assess your insurance needs based on your financial situation, dependents, lifestyle, and future goals. Determine what risks you need to protect against and the appropriate amount of coverage for each type of insurance, such as life insurance, health insurance, disability insurance, or property and casualty insurance.

2. Policy Features and Benefits:

Understand the features, benefits, and limitations of the insurance policy. Review the coverage details, exclusions, conditions, and any optional riders or endorsements available to customize your coverage to suit your needs.

3. Premiums and Affordability:

Evaluate the cost of the insurance premiums and ensure they fit within your budget. Compare quotes from multiple insurers to find competitive rates while maintaining adequate coverage. Consider the long-term affordability of the premiums, especially for policies with recurring payments.

4. Financial Strength and Reputation of the Insurer:

Choose a reputable insurance company with a strong financial rating and a history of reliability, prompt claims settlement, and excellent customer service. Research the insurer's financial strength ratings from independent rating agencies like A.M. Best, Standard & Poor's, or Moody's to assess their stability and ability to fulfil their obligations. The Government of India backs the Life Insurance Corporation of India, so in India that is probably the safest.

5. Policy Terms and Conditions:

Read and understand the policy terms, conditions, and obligations before purchasing insurance. Pay attention to factors such as coverage limits, deductibles, waiting periods, exclusions, renewal provisions, cancellation policies, and any penalties for lapses or non-payment.

6. Claims Process and Customer Service:

Evaluate the insurer's claims process, responsiveness, and customer service quality. Choose an insurer known for fair and efficient claims handling, accessible customer support, and transparency in communication.

7. Professional Advice:

Consider seeking guidance from a qualified insurance agent, financial advisor, or insurance specialist who can assess your insurance needs, explain your options, and help you select suitable insurance coverage tailored to your circumstances and objectives.

While insurance can provide valuable protection and financial security, it is essential to approach insurance purchases thoughtfully, understand the terms and conditions of the policies, and regularly review your coverage to ensure it remains adequate and appropriate for your changing needs.

Pension plans and how are they useful?

Pension plans, also known as retirement plans or superannuation schemes in some regions, are financial arrangements designed to provide income and financial security to individuals during their retirement years. These plans are typically sponsored by employers, government entities, or private financial institutions and offer a structured way for individuals to save and invest for retirement. Pension plans aim to replace a portion of an individual's pre-retirement income once they stop working.

There are several types of pension plans, each with its own features and characteristics:

1. Defined Benefit Pension Plans:

In a defined benefit plan, the employer guarantees a specific retirement benefit based on factors such as the employee's salary, years of service, and a predetermined formula. The employer bears the investment and longevity risks, and the benefit amount is typically fixed or based on a set formula.

2. Defined Contribution Pension Plans:

In a defined contribution plan, both the employer and/or the employee contribute to the plan, usually through regular payroll deductions. The contributions are invested in a range of investment options chosen by the participant, such as stocks, bonds, mutual funds, or exchange-traded funds (ETFs). The retirement benefit is based on the contributions made and the investment returns earned. Examples of defined contribution plans include the Public Provident Fund and the National Pension Scheme (NPS) in India, 401(k) plans in the United States, and Registered Retirement Savings Plans (RRSPs) in Canada.

3. Government-Sponsored Pension Plans:

Many countries have government-sponsored pension plans to provide retirement benefits to eligible citizens. These plans, such as Social Security in the United States, the Canada Pension Plan (CPP), or the National Pension System (NPS) in India, may be funded through payroll taxes, contributions from employers and employees, or government subsidies.

4. Individual Retirement Accounts (IRAs) and Personal Pension Plans:

Individuals can also set up individual retirement accounts (IRAs) or personal pension plans to save for retirement outside of employer-sponsored plans. These plans offer tax advantages and a range of investment options, allowing individuals to build a retirement nest egg independently.

Pension plans play a crucial role in retirement planning by helping individuals accumulate savings, invest for the future, and ensure financial security during their retirement years. They provide a structured framework for retirement savings, offer tax advantages, and may include employer contributions or incentives to encourage participation. It is essential for individuals to understand the features, benefits, and limitations of pension plans and to actively take part in saving and planning for retirement to achieve their long-term financial goals.

The Public Provident Fund (PPF) scheme in India

This is a long-term savings and investment scheme introduced by the Indian government to encourage individuals to save for their retirement and build a financial safety net. PPF is one of the most popular and tax-efficient investment options available to Indian residents. It uses the power of compounding to great effect in creating a corpus for later in life.

Here are the key features of the Public Provident Fund scheme:

1. Government-backed Scheme:

PPF is a government-backed investment scheme introduced by the Ministry of Finance, the Government of India. It is governed by the Public Provident Fund Act, 1968. This means it is one of the safest investments you can make.

2. Long-Term Investment:

PPF is designed as a long-term investment, with a maturity period of 15 years. However, investors have the option to extend the investment in blocks of five years indefinitely after the initial maturity period.

3. Tax Benefits:

- Contributions made to PPF accounts are eligible for tax deductions under Section 80C of the Income Tax Act, up to a specified limit. The interest earned and the maturity proceeds are tax free.

4. Interest rate

The interest rate on PPF accounts is set by the government and is typically higher than other fixed-income investment options. The interest rate is subject to revision by the government on a quarterly basis but remains fixed for each quarter for all investments made during that period.

5. Minimum and Maximum Contribution:

Investors can open a PPF account with a minimum deposit amount, which may vary from time to time as determined by the government. There is a maximum limit on the total contribution that can be made to a PPF account in a fiscal year, which is also determined by the government.

6. Flexibility:

PPF accounts offer flexibility in terms of contribution frequency and amount. Investors can make contributions through lump-sum deposits or regular monthly instalments.

7. Loan Facility:

PPF account holders are eligible to avail of loans against their PPF balances from the third fiscal year up to the sixth fiscal year of opening the account. The loan amount is limited to a specified percentage of the balance available in the PPF account.

8. Withdrawal and Premature Closure:

Partial withdrawals are permitted from the seventh fiscal year onwards, subject to certain conditions and limitations. Premature closure of PPF accounts is allowed in specific circumstances, such as medical emergencies or higher education expenses.

9. Nomination Facility:

PPF account holders can nominate one or more individuals to receive the proceeds of the PPF account in the event of the account holder's demise.

The Public Provident Fund scheme offers a secure and tax-efficient avenue for long-term savings and investment, making it a popular choice among Indian investors for retirement planning and wealth accumulation.

The National Pension Scheme. (NPS)

The National Pension System (NPS) is a voluntary, contributory pension scheme launched by the Government of India to provide retirement income to citizens.

It is regulated and administered by the Pension Fund Regulatory and Development Authority (PFRDA), established by the government to oversee and regulate pension funds in India. Here are the key features of the National Pension Scheme:

1. Voluntary Participation:

NPS is open to all Indian citizens, including residents and non-residents, aged between 18 and 65 years. It is also available to corporate entities for their employees.

2. Tiered Structure:

NPS operates under a two-tiered structure comprising Tier-I and Tier-II accounts.

Tier-I is the primary retirement account with restrictions on withdrawals, while Tier-II is an optional savings account with more flexibility for withdrawals.

3. Contributions:

In Tier-I, subscribers are required to make regular contributions towards their retirement savings. These contributions are invested in various pension funds of their choice, managed by Pension Fund Managers (PFMs) appointed by the PFRDA. In Tier-II, contributions are voluntary and can be made at the subscriber's discretion.

4. Investment Options:

NPS offers a range of investment options to suit different risk appetites and preferences. Subscribers can choose from various asset classes, including equity, corporate bonds, government securities, and alternative investments like real estate investment trusts (REITs) and infrastructure investment trusts (InvITs).

5. Tax Benefits:

- Contributions made towards NPS are eligible for tax deductions under Section 80CCD of the Income Tax Act, subject to certain limits. Additionally, contributions made by employers towards employees' NPS accounts are eligible for tax deductions under Section 80CCD (2).

6. Portability:

NPS accounts are portable across employers and locations, allowing subscribers to continue their contributions and investments even if they change jobs or relocate. Subscribers can also switch between PFMs and investment options as per their preferences.

7. Retirement Benefits:

Upon retirement or reaching the age of sixty, subscribers can withdraw a portion of their accumulated NPS corpus as a lump sum and use the remaining amount to purchase an annuity to receive regular pension income. Subscribers also have the option to defer withdrawals and continue their investments until the age of seventy.

8. Exit and

NPS offers flexibility in withdrawals, allowing subscribers to make partial withdrawals for specific purposes like higher education, marriage, or medical emergencies, subject to certain conditions.

The National Pension System aims to provide individuals with a sustainable retirement income stream and promote long-term savings and investment habits. It offers tax benefits, investment flexibility, and portability, making it an attractive retirement planning option for Indian citizens.

What is the National Savings Scheme (NSS) and Kisan Vikas Patra (KVP)?

These are two popular savings and investment schemes offered by the Government of India through the Department of Posts and authorized banks. Both schemes aim to promote savings and provide safe investment options for individuals across different income groups. Here is an overview of each:

1. National Savings Scheme (NSS):

The National Savings Scheme encompasses various small savings schemes offered by the Government of India, including Public Provident Fund (PPF), Senior Citizens Savings Scheme (SCSS), Sukanya Samriddhi Yojana (SSY), National Savings Certificate (NSC), and others.

These schemes offer attractive interest rates, tax benefits, and capital protection to investors. They cater to different financial goals and risk profiles, such as retirement planning, tax savings, education funding, and wealth accumulation.

NSS schemes are available through designated post offices, public sector banks, and authorized agents across India. They offer a secure and convenient way for individuals to save and invest, with minimal risk and government backing.

1. Kisan Vikas Patra (KVP):

Kisan Vikas Patra is a savings certificate scheme launched by the Government of India to encourage small farmers and individuals to invest in a secure and hassle-free manner. It is popular among rural investors and individuals seeking low-risk investment options.

KVP certificates are available in various denominations, starting from as low as ₹1,000, with no upper limit on investment. The certificates have a fixed maturity period, typically ranging from 124 months (approximately 10 years) to 118 months (approximately 9 years and 10 months), depending on the prevailing interest rate.

KVP certificates offer a guaranteed rate of return, compounded annually, which is determined by the government. The interest earned is taxable, but there is no TDS (Tax Deducted at Source) on the interest.

KVP certificates can be encashed prematurely after a specified lock-in period, subject to certain conditions and penalties. They can also be transferred from one person to another or pledged as security for loans.

Both the National Savings Scheme and Kisan Vikas Patra provide individuals with safe and accessible investment options, offering assured returns and liquidity. They are suitable for conservative investors seeking capital protection and steady returns over the medium to the long term. However, investors should assess their investment objectives, risk tolerance, and liquidity needs before choosing the most appropriate savings scheme for their financial goals.

How can you invest in the stock market?

Investing in the stock market in India and in most other countries can be done online through various avenues, each offering various levels of access, control, and convenience. Here are some common methods for investing in the Indian stock market:

1. Direct Equity Investment:

Direct equity investment involves buying and holding shares of individual companies listed on stock exchanges like the National Stock Exchange (NSE) or the Bombay Stock Exchange (BSE). Investors can open a brokerage account with a registered stockbroker, such as a full-service broker or a discount broker, and place buy orders for specific stocks through the broker's trading platform.

Direct equity investment offers investors full control over their investment decisions, allowing them to research and select individual stocks based on their preferences, risk tolerance, and investment objectives.

2. Mutual Funds:

Mutual funds pool money from multiple investors to invest in a diversified portfolio of stocks, bonds, or other securities. In India, there are several types of mutual funds, including equity funds, debt funds, hybrid funds, etc.

Investors can invest in mutual funds through asset management companies (AMCs) or mutual fund distributors. Mutual funds offer diversification, professional management, and convenience for investors who prefer a hands-off approach to investing in the stock market.

3. Exchange-Traded Funds (ETFs):

ETFs are investment funds that trade on stock exchanges, like individual stocks. They typically track a specific index, sector, commodity, or asset class. In India, ETFs are available for various indices like Nifty 50.

Investors can buy and sell ETF units through their brokerage accounts, like stocks. ETFs offer diversification, liquidity, and lower expense ratios compared to actively managed mutual funds.

4. Initial Public Offerings (IPOs):

IPOs are the process through which a company offers its shares to the public for the first time. Investors can take part in IPOs by applying for shares through their brokerage accounts or through online platforms provided by banks or financial institutions.

Investing in IPOs allows investors to buy shares of newly listed companies at the offering price, potentially benefiting from capital appreciation if the company performs well post-listing.

5. Employee Stock Ownership Plans (ESOPs) and Employee Stock Purchase Plans (ESPPs):

ESOPs and ESPPs are employee benefit programs that allow employees of a company to gain shares of their employer's stock at a discounted price or as part of their compensation package. Employees can take part in these plans through their employers' designated processes.

Before investing in the stock market, it is essential to conduct thorough research, understand the risks involved, and consider factors such as investment objectives, risk tolerance, and time horizon. Investors should ensure they have a demat account for holding shares in electronic form and a trading account for executing buy and sell orders. Seeking advice from a qualified financial advisor can also help investors make informed investment decisions based on their individual circumstances and goals.

Mutual Funds

Mutual funds are investment vehicles that pool money from multiple investors to invest in a diversified portfolio of stocks, bonds, or other securities managed by professional fund managers. Here are the key characteristics, pros, and cons of mutual funds:

Pros:

1. Diversification:

Mutual funds offer investors access to a diversified portfolio of securities, which helps spread investment risk across different asset classes, industries, and regions. Diversification can help reduce the impact of adverse events affecting any single investment.

2. Professional Management:

Mutual funds are managed by experienced and qualified fund managers who make investment decisions on behalf of investors. These professionals conduct research, analyse market trends, and actively manage the portfolio to achieve the fund's investment objectives.

3. Accessibility:

Mutual funds are accessible to investors with varying levels of investment capital. Investors can start investing in mutual funds with lesser amounts, making them suitable for retail investors who may not have the resources to build a diversified portfolio of individual securities.

4. Liquidity:

Mutual funds offer liquidity, allowing investors to buy and sell fund units on any business day at the fund's net asset value (NAV). This provides flexibility for investors to access their investment capital when needed, without incurring significant transaction costs.

5. Transparency:

Mutual funds provide regular updates and disclosures about their portfolio holdings, performance, expenses, and investment strategies. Investors have access to comprehensive information to make informed decisions and monitor their investments.

6. Cost-Effective:

Mutual funds typically have lower investment costs compared to investing directly in individual securities. The pooling of assets allows mutual funds to achieve economies of scale, reducing transaction costs and administrative expenses for investors.

Cons:

1. Management Fees:

Mutual funds charge management fees and other expenses, such as operating expenses and administrative fees, which are deducted from the fund's assets. While these fees compensate fund managers for their expertise and services, they can erode overall returns.

2. Market Risks:

Mutual funds are subject to market risks, including fluctuations in stock prices, interest rates, currency exchange rates, and economic conditions. Despite diversification, the value of mutual fund investments can decline due to adverse market movements. The brochure put out may show a rosy picture, but we should know that this is to sell the fund, and the fine print will state that investments are subject to market risks. This means if the fund manager does not invest properly, you will lose the money and not the fund manager. If a fund manager is managing too many funds, it is better to avoid as he or she may not have time to adequately manage the fund.

3. Lack of Control:

Mutual fund investors delegate investment decisions to fund managers, relinquishing direct control over the selection and timing of individual securities. Investors must trust the fund manager's expertise and adhere to the fund's investment objectives and strategies.

4. Tax Implications:

Mutual fund investments may have tax implications, including capital gains taxes on redemption or the sale of fund units and dividend distribution taxes on income generated by the fund. Investors should consider the tax consequences of mutual fund investments based on their individual tax situations.

5. Potential for Underperformance:

Despite professional management, mutual funds may underperform their benchmarks or fail to meet investors' expectations due to numerous factors, including market conditions, fund manager decisions, and investment style drift.

Overall, mutual funds offer a convenient and accessible way for investors to build diversified investment portfolios, achieve their financial goals, and navigate the complexities of the financial markets. However, investors should carefully assess the pros and cons of mutual funds and consider factors such as investment objectives, risk tolerance, time horizon, and fund expenses before making investment decisions.

My name is Bond, Treasury Bond!

Bonds and treasury notes

These are types of fixed-income securities issued by governments, corporations, or other entities to raise capital. They represent a form of debt where the issuer borrows money from investors and promises to repay the principal amount, along with periodic interest payments over a specified period. Here is an overview of bonds and treasury notes:

Bonds:

1. Definition:

Bonds are debt securities issued by governments, municipalities, corporations, or other entities to raise funds for various purposes, such as financing infrastructure projects, funding operations, or expanding business activities.

When investors buy bonds, they are lending money to the issuer in exchange for regular interest payments, known as coupon payments, and the repayment of the principal amount at maturity.

2. Features:

Bonds have a fixed maturity date, which is the date when the issuer repays the principal amount to investors. Maturities can range from short-term (less than one year) to long-term (over 30 years).

Bonds pay periodic interest payments, typically semi-annually or annually, based on the coupon rate, which is the fixed or floating interest rate determined at the time of issuance.

Bonds may be issued in various denominations, ranging from small denominations accessible to retail investors to large denominations targeted at institutional investors.

3. Types of Bonds:

Government Bonds: Issued by national governments, such as Treasury bonds in the United States or the Government of India bonds.

Corporate Bonds: Issued by corporations to raise capital for business operations or expansion.

Municipal Bonds: Issued by state or local governments to finance public projects like roads, schools, or utilities.

Treasury Notes:

1. Definition:

Treasury notes, also known as T-notes, are medium-term debt securities issued by the government through the Department of the Treasury. They represent a promise to repay the principal amount at maturity and pay fixed or floating interest payments semi-annually until maturity.

2. Features:

Treasury notes have fixed maturities ranging from two to ten years, making them suitable for investors seeking intermediate-term investments with relatively predictable cash flows.

Like other Treasury securities, T-notes are low-risk investments due to the creditworthiness of the government, making them attractive to investors seeking safety and income.

3. Interest Payments:

Treasury notes pay semi-annual interest payments to investors based on the coupon rate determined at the time of issuance. The interest payments are exempt from state and local taxes but are subject to federal or central income tax.

4. Liquidity:

Treasury notes are highly liquid investments, as they can be bought and sold on the secondary market through brokerage firms, banks, or financial institutions. Investors can easily access their investment capital by selling T-notes before maturity.

In summary, bonds and treasury notes are fixed-income securities that offer investors a predictable stream of income through periodic interest payments and the repayment of the principal amount at maturity. They provide diversification, income, and capital preservation benefits to investors seeking to balance risk and return in their investment portfolios.

What are IPOs?

An Initial Public Offering (IPO) is the process through which a private company offers its shares to the public for the first time, allowing it to raise capital from external investors. By conducting an IPO, a company transitions from being privately owned to being publicly traded, with its shares listed on a stock exchange for trading by investors. Here is an overview of the IPO process and its key components.

1. Preparation:

Before initiating an IPO, the company typically undergoes extensive preparation, including financial audits, due diligence, and regulatory compliance checks. The company engages investment banks, also known as underwriters, to help facilitate the offering and advice on pricing, timing, and market conditions.

2. Filing:

The company files a registration statement, known as the prospectus, with the securities regulator in the area where it intends to offer its shares. The prospectus contains detailed information about the company's business, financials, operations, risks, and proposed terms of the offering.

3. Review and Approval:

The securities regulator reviews the prospectus to ensure compliance with applicable securities laws and regulations. Once the regulator approves the offering, the company receives a registration statement, allowing it to proceed with the IPO.

4. Marketing and Roadshow:

- The company, along with its underwriters, conducts a marketing campaign to generate interest from potential investors. This often includes a roadshow, where company executives present the investment opportunity to institutional investors, analysts, and the media, highlighting the company's growth prospects, competitive advantages, and investment merits.

5. Pricing:

- Based on feedback from investors and market conditions, the company and its underwriters determine the IPO price, also known as the offering price or the issue price. The IPO price is typically set at a level that balances the company's valuation, investor demand, and market expectations.

6. Allocation and Allotment:

On the day of the IPO, investors submit their orders to purchase shares at the offering price through their brokerage firms or investment banks. The underwriters allocate shares to investors based on demand, investor profiles, and other factors. Once the allocation process is completed, the shares are allotted to investors.

7. Trading:

After the shares are allocated and allotted, they are listed on a stock exchange for trading by investors. The first day of trading, known as the IPO day or the listing day, is often characterized by high volatility as investors buy and sell shares based on market sentiment and price movements.

8. Post-IPO:

Following the IPO, the company becomes subject to regulatory reporting requirements and disclosure obligations as a publicly traded company. It must provide regular updates on its financial performance, operations, and other material developments to shareholders and the public.

An IPO provides companies with access to public capital markets, enhances liquidity for existing shareholders, raises the company's profile, and can facilitate future growth opportunities through additional financing. However, it also involves significant regulatory scrutiny, compliance costs, and the potential for market volatility and investor expectations.

A look at Debentures are debt instruments.

These are issued by companies or governments to raise capital from investors. When an investor purchases a debenture, they are lending money to the issuer in exchange for a promise to repay the principal amount at maturity and periodic interest payments over the life of the debenture. Unlike shares, debentures do not represent ownership in the company and typically rank higher in terms of priority for repayment in the event of bankruptcy or liquidation.

Here are the different types of debentures:

1. Secured Debentures:

Secured debentures are backed by specific assets or collateral pledged by the issuer as security for the repayment of the debenture holders. In the event of default, secured debenture holders have a claim on the underlying assets to recover their investment.

2. Unsecured Debentures (or Naked Debentures):

Unsecured debentures, also known as naked debentures or simple debentures, are not backed by any specific collateral. Instead, they are supported only by the general creditworthiness and financial standing of the issuer. Unsecured debenture holders rank lower in priority for repayment compared to secured debenture holders in case of default.

3. Convertible Debentures:

- Convertible debentures give debenture holders the option to convert their debentures into equity shares of the issuing company after a specified period or under certain conditions. This provides investors with the opportunity to take part in any potential upside in the company's share price while retaining the fixed-income characteristics of the debenture.

4. Non-Convertible Debentures (NCDs):

Non-convertible debentures do not carry the option of conversion into equity shares. They remain as debt instruments throughout their tenure, providing fixed interest payments to debenture holders until maturity. NCDs are typically issued with specific terms, such as coupon rate, maturity period, and repayment terms.

5. Perpetual

Perpetual debentures, also known as perpetual bonds or irredeemable debentures, have no fixed maturity date. They pay periodic interest indefinitely, with no obligation for the issuer to repay the principal amount. Perpetual debenture holders may be able to redeem their debentures at specified intervals or under certain conditions.

6. Callable Debentures:

Callable debentures give the issuer the right to redeem the debentures before their maturity date, usually at a predetermined call price or redemption price. Issuers typically exercise this option when prevailing interest rates are lower than the coupon rate on the debentures, allowing them to refinance their debt at a lower cost.

7. Fixed-Rate Debentures:

- Fixed-rate debentures pay a predetermined fixed rate of interest throughout their tenure, providing investors with predictable cash flows. The interest rate remains constant regardless of changes in market interest rates.

8. Floating-Rate Debentures:

Floating-rate debentures have a variable interest rate that adjusts periodically based on changes in a specified benchmark rate, such as the prevailing market interest rate or a reference rate like LIBOR (London Interbank Offered Rate). Floating-rate debentures provide protection against interest rate risk, as the interest payments fluctuate with prevailing market conditions.

Debentures offer investors a fixed-income investment option with varying features and characteristics to suit different investment objectives, risk profiles, and preferences. Investors should carefully consider the terms and conditions of debentures, as well as the creditworthiness of the issuer, before investing in these instruments.

Before making any investment, it is important to take certain precautions to protect your capital and make informed decisions. Here are some key precautions to consider:

1. Set Clear Investment Goals:

Define your investment objectives, such as capital preservation, income generation, wealth accumulation, or retirement planning. Establishing clear goals will help guide your investment decisions and asset allocation.

2. Assess Risk Tolerance:

Evaluate your risk tolerance, which refers to your ability and willingness to withstand fluctuations in the value of your investments. Consider factors such as your investment period, financial situation, income stability, and emotional temperament.

3. Diversify Your Portfolio:

Diversification is a key risk management strategy that involves spreading your investments across different asset classes, sectors, regions, and investment types. Diversified portfolios are less susceptible to the impact of adverse events affecting any single investment.

4. Conduct Research:

Thoroughly research potential investment opportunities, including the underlying assets, market conditions, industry trends, financial performance, and risks associated with each investment. Use reputable sources of information and seek advice from qualified financial professionals if needed.

5. Understand Investment Products:

Understand the features, terms, and risks associated with different investment products, such as stocks, bonds, mutual funds, ETFs, real estate, and alternative investments. Consider how each investment aligns with your goals, risk tolerance, and investment strategy. Do not go by the sales story offered by the company or person selling these products. Check it yourself.

6. Consider Costs and Fees:

Consider the costs and fees associated with investing, including brokerage commissions, management fees, administrative expenses, and taxes. Minimizing investment costs can help enhance your overall returns. Always look if there are hidden costs.

7. Monitor Your Investments:

Regularly monitor your investment portfolio and track performance against your goals and benchmarks. Review your asset allocation, rebalance as needed, and adjust based on changing market conditions or personal circumstances.

While investing offers the potential for growth and wealth accumulation, it also involves certain risks that investors should know:

1. Market Risk:

- Market risk, also known as systematic risk, refers to the risk of losses due to broad market movements, such as economic downturns, geopolitical events, interest rate changes, or fluctuations in stock prices and bond yields.

2. Credit Risk:

Credit risk, or default risk, is the risk that the issuer of a debt security, such as a bond or debenture, may fail to make interest payments or repay the principal amount on time. Credit risk is higher for lower-rated or non-investment-grade securities.

3. Inflation Risk:

Inflation risk is the risk that the purchasing power of your investment returns may be eroded over time due to inflationary pressures. Investments with fixed returns, such as bonds or cash equivalents, are particularly vulnerable to inflation risk.

1. Liquidity Risk: Liquidity risk is the risk that you may not be able to sell your investments quickly or at fair market prices, especially during periods of market stress or illiquidity. Investments in less liquid assets, such as real estate or certain types of bonds, may be subject to liquidity risk.
2. Interest Rate Risk:

Interest rate risk is the risk that changes in prevailing interest rates may affect the value of fixed-income securities, such as bonds or debentures. Bond prices and yields move inversely, meaning that rising interest rates can lead to declines in bond prices and vice versa.

6. Currency Risk: Currency risk, or exchange rate risk, is the risk that fluctuations in foreign exchange rates may impact the value of investments denominated in foreign currencies. Currency risk is relevant for international investments or assets held in foreign currencies.

There is no investment that is entirely risk free, as all investments carry some level of risk. However, some investment options are considered safer or more conservative than others, depending on your investment goals and risk tolerance:

1. Fixed-Income Securities:

Fixed-income securities, such as government bonds, treasury bills, and high-quality corporate bonds, are often considered safer investments due to their predictable income streams and lower volatility compared to stocks.

2. Savings Accounts and Certificates of Deposit (CDs):

Savings accounts and CDs offered by banks provide a safer and more liquid option for preserving capital and earning a modest return. These investments are insured by government deposit insurance schemes, but only to a limited extent.

3. Money Market Funds: Money market funds invest in short-term, high-quality debt securities, such as treasury bills and commercial paper, with the goal of preserving capital and maintaining liquidity. Money market funds are considered relatively safe investments with a low risk of principal loss.

4. Index Funds and ETFs:

Index funds and exchange-traded funds (ETFs) that track broad market indices, such as the NIFTY, the SENSEX, S&P 500, or the FTSE 100, offer diversified exposure to the stock market at a relatively low cost. These passive investment vehicles provide broad market exposure and can help mitigate individual stock risk.

5. Blue-Chip Stocks:

Blue-chip stocks are shares of large, well-established companies with strong financial fundamentals, stable earnings, and a history of dividend payments. Investing in blue-chip stocks can provide exposure to equities with lower volatility and less risk compared to smaller or speculative companies.

Ultimately, the safest investment depends on your individual financial situation, investment goals, time horizon, and risk tolerance. It is important to carefully assess the risks and potential rewards of each investment option and construct a well-diversified portfolio that aligns with your objectives and preferences. Consider consulting with a qualified financial advisor to help develop an appropriate investment strategy tailored to your needs.

Investment Plans.

An investment plan is a systematic approach to allocating your financial resources across different investment vehicles based on your financial goals, risk tolerance, time horizon, and other personal factors. The goal of an investment plan is to maximize returns while minimizing risk and achieving your financial objectives.

Here are some suggested ideal investments plan based on different age groups:

1. Young Adults (20s to early 30s):

Financial Goals: Establish an emergency fund, pay off high-interest debt, save for short-term goals (e.g., travel, education), and start building long-term wealth (e.g., retirement, homeownership).

Investment Strategy:

Allocate a portion of savings to a high-yield savings account or money market fund for the emergency fund.

Focus on paying off high-interest debt, such as credit card debt or student loans, to reduce financial liabilities.

Diversify investments across a mix of growth-oriented assets, such as stocks or equity mutual funds, to capitalize on long-term growth potential.

Consider investing in tax-efficient investment vehicles, like NPS, PPF, to benefit from tax-free growth and withdrawals in retirement.

Take advantage of compounding by reinvesting dividends and regularly contributing to investment accounts.

2. Midlife (Late 30s to 50s):

Financial Goals: Continue building wealth for retirement, saving for children's education, paying off remaining debt, and protecting assets with insurance.

Investment Strategy:

Review and adjust asset allocation based on changing financial goals, risk tolerance, and market conditions.

Increase contributions to retirement accounts to maximize tax advantages and speed up wealth accumulation.

Consider diversifying investments across a mix of asset classes, including stocks, bonds, real estate, and alternative investments, to reduce portfolio volatility.

Allocate a portion of savings to college savings plans or other education savings accounts to fund children's education expenses.

Review and update insurance coverage, including life insurance, disability insurance, and long-term care insurance, to protect against unexpected events.

3. Pre-Retirement (Late 50s to early 60s):

Financial Goals: Transition from wealth accumulation to wealth preservation, evaluate retirement readiness, develop a retirement income plan, and consider downsizing expenses.

Investment Strategy:

Shift focus from growth-oriented investments to more conservative assets, such as bonds, cash equivalents, and dividend-paying stocks, to reduce portfolio volatility and preserve capital.

Evaluate retirement accounts and pension benefits to determine retirement income sources and withdrawal strategies.

Consider purchasing immediate annuities or deferred annuities to generate guaranteed income streams in retirement.

Review and update estate planning documents, including wills, trusts, and powers of attorney, to ensure assets are transferred according to your wishes and minimize estate taxes.

Explore long-term care insurance options to cover potential healthcare expenses in retirement.

4. Retirement (60s and beyond):

Financial Goals: Generate retirement income, manage expenses, monitor investment performance, and plan for potential healthcare costs and long-term care needs.

Investment Strategy:

Implement a retirement income strategy that balances income needs, investment returns, and longevity risk, considering factors such as Social Security benefits, pension payments, and portfolio withdrawals.

Continuously monitor investment portfolios and adjust asset allocation as needed to maintain income levels, mitigate inflation risk, and preserve purchasing power in retirement.

Consider a "bucket" approach to retirement income planning, segregating assets into different buckets based on short-term, medium-term, and long-term income needs.

Plan for potential healthcare expenses and long-term care needs by exploring Medicare options, supplemental insurance coverage, and long-term care insurance solutions.

Review and update estate planning documents periodically to reflect changes in personal circumstances, family dynamics, and financial goals.

It is important to note that investment plans should be flexible and adaptable to changing circumstances, market conditions, and life events. Regularly review and adjust your investment plan as needed to stay on track toward achieving your financial objectives and maintaining financial security at every stage of life. Additionally, consider consulting with a qualified financial advisor to develop a personalized investment strategy tailored to your individual needs and goals.

A Systematic Investment Plan (SIP)

A SIP is an investment strategy that allows investors to regularly invest a fixed amount of money in mutual funds or other investment vehicles at predetermined intervals, typically monthly or quarterly. SIPs offer a disciplined and systematic approach to investing, helping investors accumulate wealth over time through the power of compounding. Here's how SIP works and its pros and cons:

How SIP Works:

1. Regular Investments: Investors commit to investing a fixed amount of money at regular intervals, such as monthly or quarterly.

2. Automatic Deductions: The predetermined investment amount is automatically deducted from the investor's bank account and invested in the chosen mutual fund scheme.

3. Rupee Cost Averaging: SIPs facilitate rupee cost averaging, whereby investors buy more units of the mutual fund when prices are low and fewer units when prices are high. This helps reduce the average cost per unit over time.

4. Long-Term Approach: SIPs encourage a long-term investment horizon, allowing investors to benefit from the compounding effect over time and ride out market volatility.

Pros of SIP:

1. Disciplined Investing: SIPs promote disciplined investing habits by automating the investment process and eliminating the need for the timing of the market.

2. Rupee Cost Averaging: SIPs help investors mitigate the impact of market volatility by spreading investments over time and benefiting from rupee cost averaging.

3. Convenience: SIPs are convenient and hassle-free, as investors can set up automatic deductions from their bank accounts and invest without the need for frequent monitoring or intervention.

4. Affordability: SIPs allow investors to invest with lesser amounts, making it accessible to a wide range of investors, including those with limited financial resources.

5. Compounding Benefits: SIPs harness the power of compounding, where returns generated on investments are reinvested to generate additional returns over time, leading to exponential growth in wealth.

Cons of SIP:

1. Market Risk: SIPs are subject to market risk, and investors may experience fluctuations in the value of their investments due to changes in market conditions, economic factors, or geopolitical events.

2. No Timing Advantage: While SIPs help mitigate the risk of timing the market, they also eliminate the potential for capitalizing on market opportunities or timing market highs and lows.

3. Fixed Commitment: Investors commit to investing a fixed amount regularly through SIPs, which may not be suitable for those with fluctuating income or uncertain cash flows.

4. Limited Flexibility: SIPs offer limited flexibility in terms of investment amounts and timing, as investors typically cannot change or suspend SIPs without penalties or restrictions.

Overall, SIPs are an effective and convenient investment strategy for investors looking to build wealth gradually over time, mitigate market risk, and benefit from the power of compounding. However, investors should carefully consider their investment goals, risk tolerance, and financial circumstances before implementing SIPs and regularly review their investment portfolios to ensure alignment with their objectives.

Blue chip stocks and penny stocks.

These represent two contrasting categories of stocks based on their characteristics, market capitalization, and investment profiles:

Blue Chip Stocks:

Blue chip stocks refer to shares of well-established, financially sound companies with a long history of stable earnings, strong balance sheets, and reputable business operations.

Characteristics of Blue-Chip Stocks:

1. Large Market Capitalization: Blue chip companies typically have large market capitalizations, representing the total value of all outstanding shares, often exceeding billions of dollars.

2. Industry Leaders: Blue chip companies are often leaders in their respective industries, with dominant market positions, recognizable brand names, and sustainable competitive advantages.

3. Stable Dividend Payments: Blue chip stocks pay regular dividends to shareholders, reflecting their stable earnings, consistent cash flows, and commitment to returning value to investors.

4. Lower Volatility: Blue chip stocks are known for their relatively lower volatility compared to smaller or speculative stocks, making them less susceptible to abrupt price fluctuations.

Examples of Blue-Chip Stocks:

Companies like Indian Oil Corporation, Hindustan Lever Limited, Reliance Industries, Apple Inc., Microsoft Corporation, Johnson & Johnson, The Coca-Cola Company, and Procter & Gamble are considered blue chip stocks due to their strong financial performance, global presence, and investor confidence.

Penny Stocks:

Penny stocks, also known as micro-cap stocks or small-cap stocks, are shares of companies with low market capitalizations and small trading volumes, often trading at exceptionally low prices per share, typically less than Rs.100 or even lesser.

Characteristics of Penny Stocks:

1. Low Market Capitalization: Penny stocks are characterized by low market capitalizations.

2. High Volatility: Penny stocks are highly volatile and prone to price manipulation, speculative trading, and rapid price movements driven by news, rumours, or market sentiment.

3. Limited Financial Information: Many penny stock companies are unknown or have limited financial disclosures, making it challenging for investors to assess their fundamentals or evaluate their investment prospects.

4. Higher Risk: Penny stocks are high-risk investments due to their speculative nature, lack of liquidity, potential for fraud or manipulation, and greater susceptibility to adverse market conditions.

Examples of Penny Stocks:

Penny stocks are often found in emerging industries, start-up companies, or companies with uncertain prospects. Examples include early-stage biotech companies, speculative mining companies, or small technology firms with unproven business models.

In summary, blue-chip stocks are shares of large, well-established companies with strong fundamentals and lower volatility, making them suitable for conservative investors seeking stability and income.

In contrast, penny stocks are shares of smaller, speculative companies with higher risk and volatility, often favoured by aggressive traders seeking short-term gains but requiring careful consideration and due diligence due to their inherent risks. Investors should carefully assess their investment objectives, risk tolerance, and financial circumstances before considering investments in either blue chip stocks or penny stocks.

Don't miss out!

Visit the website below and you can sign up to receive emails whenever R RADHAKRISHNAN publishes a new book. There's no charge and no obligation.

https://books2read.com/r/B-A-QDEN-EVSCF

About the Author

Radhakrishnan, a seasoned traveler and storyteller, hails from Mumbai, India, and has explored various parts of the country during his three-decade-long career in a petroleum company. Being fluent in six languages has enabled him to connect with people and listen to their stories.

Passionate about narratives, Radhakrishnan has been exposed to a wide range of stories and their different versions throughout his travels, which significantly transformed his perspectives on life and India as a whole. His book, "Traveller's Tales Once upon a Time," set in the rapidly changing India of the 1970s, 1980s, and 1990s, offers captivating insights into a bygone era. With a delightful touch of humor and profound insight, these stories are sure to captivate and enchant readers.

Radhakrishnan's fascination with Indian mythology has led him to immerse himself in the ancient tales that have been passed down through generations. He heard these stories first from his parents and grandparents and later during encounters with many people during his journeys. These timeless stories embody the essence of India's soul, forming a living mythology in the ancient land. Radhakrishnan masterfully retells these tales, infusing simplicity and clarity while highlighting the invaluable life lessons they impart, lessons that remain relevant in the present day.

After retiring from Indian Oil, Radhakrishnan now dedicates his time fully to his passion for writing and traveling. His writing style is marked by simplicity, clarity, and empathy, effortlessly presenting complex ideas in concise and understandable ways. Occasionally, his emotions spill over, giving rise to stark and minimalist poetry, where profound thoughts and ideas are beautifully etched.

When not exploring India, Radhakrishnan lives in the picturesque coastal city of Cochin, Kerala, with his wife and two children. He maintains a blog titled **radhawrites.com**. Experience the artistry of Radhakrishnan's storytelling and embark on a journey through his vivid narratives, allowing yourself to be transported to the heart of India's diverse tapestry.

Read more at https://radhawrites.com.